LANGUAGES, FIRST AND LAST

Lauren Scharhag

Para mi familia, otra vez.

Contents

Paper Wasps

Peak housewife era, when television taught that
women were supposed to wear heels and a smile
to vacuum, arrange doilies, make molded
strawberry salad from a Good Housekeeping recipe.
If you didn't like it, you still had to abide it.
But she enjoyed laundry, even when she was young,
bent over a zinc tub, scrubbing clothes out on a washboard
alongside her own grandmother, who used to give her
a glass of beer as they worked (later bouts
of alcoholism notwithstanding). She always said
she associated the scents of hops and brewer's yeast
with her grandmother, and decades later,
that washboard still hung on her kitchen wall.
When she got her first electric machine, she still
hung everything out to dry, lighter fabrics semi-transparent
in the sundrenched yard, aromatic with pepper
and tomato plants, her sundress semi-transparent
as she turns, bends, lifts the fabrics to the line.
She either didn't notice or didn't think anything of
a wasp perched black and gold on the head of a clothespin,
like the old absurdity about pinheads and dancing angels,
only this one was, at best, the avenging variety, and,
at worst, batting for the other team,
with the infernal whine of its drained stained-glass wings,
that first sting white-hot as judgment, and they just
keep coming: the nest in the hollow metal post
of the clothesline, gray honeycomb scarcely visible
through the opening, and everything is light light light
until she passes out.

When she wakes, there will be ice packs for the swelling,
baking soda pastes, her then-husband with tweezers
to pluck out the stingers that broke off in her skin.
I was always amazed that she could go on after that,
hanging her laundry out to dry right up until 1987
when her last husband left her, and her demons
began to overrun her skull. Yet, somehow,
she never stopped finding godliness in clean sheets,
in the scents of bleach and fabric softener.
These are the scents I associate with her.
It took me a while to realize why her demons won.
There was no joy in her life that they
couldn't worm their way into, plant
their insidious nest, and wait to swarm.

A Feast for Mosquitoes

I love the mountains: the Blue Ridge,
the Great Smokies with their dim charcoal halos,
the aspen-crowned Rockies.
At those altitudes, I am one of the few
who breathes more easily,
relieved of the fear of insects,
arms and legs bared to the cold, clear air.

When I was three years old,
I spent a month at Children's Mercy:
sepsis from an infected mosquito bite.
I had to endure shots thrice daily;
but even at that age, I paid attention
to what preceded the pain.
I learned the rounds, and one day,
when I knew the doctor and his hypodermic
was imminent, I locked myself in the bathroom.
I was afraid of the dark, and too small
to reach the light switch,
but I refused to come out.
A janitor was summoned with a master key.
It took three nurses to drag me back
to the bed and hold me down.
As I struggled, my grandfather's face appeared
above me, locked in a grim acceptance.
It was the same look he got whenever
he dug splinters out from under my skin
with his pocketknife, or that time

I stepped in broken glass and left a trail
of bloody footprints up 21st.

All my life, people have joked
that my blood must be sweet,
and it's true that mosquitoes
have discriminating taste.
The moment I step out-of-doors,
a brown cloud descends,
necessitating long sleeves and jeans
despite the heat.

Once, just walking
to the next-door neighbor's house,
I garnered eighteen bites.
Once, I wore sandals
for an evening stroll,
and my feet were so ravaged,
I couldn't wear shoes for a week.

Every year, I wonder if my body
has changed enough for them
to move on, and every spring,
I get my answer in the form
of itchy red welts.

But I get some of my own back:
keeping cans of foul aerosols,
putting up bat houses,
releasing spiders into the garden,
and lighting fat, pungent pillars of citronella
while offering a prayer to whatever patron saint
delivers us from bloodsuckers.

Abuela

She sits
I stand
At the kitchen table
The bowl of water where she
Wets her fingers,
Yanking my locks into sleek submission,
No wisp allowed to escape.
She bears down hard
With the heavy, stiff-bristle brush,
The one she spanks us with. *Cállate ya.*
You got a soft head. You need to toughen up.
You can't go around looking *toda greñuda.*

A proponent of the simple rubber band as hair accessory,
She collected them on a doorknob: red, blue, putty.
More likely than not, my braid and ponytail holders had come
Wrapped around that morning's paper.
No matter how carefully we worked them out
They always took great snarls of our hair with them.
Freshly liberated, our scalps tingled.
We took aim and shot the ratty bands at each other,
Our tresses, pleated from their confinement,
Nevertheless flowed behind us as we ran
Barefoot among the broken beer bottles.

She was also partial to the ball ponytail holders
Like the black girls down the street wore.
Fifty-nine cents for a pack at TG&Y,
The kind that could snap and brain you,

Pinging off your skull like BBs fired from an air rifle.
Not enough to cause any real damage,
But enough to make your eyes water.

We learn practically in utero
That pain is beauty,
But pain is also a primer,
Preparing us for life in general
And womanhood in particular.

But not all of us seem to know
That you don't have to sit still
While life grabs you by the hair,
(Short or otherwise)
And tries to throttle you into submission.
I know it feels like love,
Like the hands of your *abuela,*
But I promise you, it isn't.

The difference is your *abuela's* hands
Sought only to give you beauty
While the others want only to take from you
All that it has to give.

Deep Creek

The Great Smokies, cool even in August,
we hiked its trails lined with mountain laurel,
beheld its many waterfalls. We caught the end
of the bee-balm, the jewel weed.
We went inner tubing, drifting for miles
through the green-gold afternoon,
limbs dangling like leaf stems over the sides.
I learned real quick that even these small rapids
could knock you from your rubber mount.
The current pulled me down,
dragged me along the rocks at the bottom.
Gasping and bleeding, I dog-paddled over to retrieve my tube
from the shallows and went on.
Eventually, the water broadened and grew quiet.
I lay back, weightless beneath the hemlock and sourwood.
The water had claimed a great deal of my skin,
some fingernails, even my silver ring.
So when I got out, I lined my pockets with river stones.
Seemed only fair.

Jesus Flicks

Summer and church-sponsored
picnics in the park:
webbed folding chairs of
scratchy plastics and hard aluminum,
mounds of hot dogs,
red coolers full of pop,
pitchers of neon-colored sour drinks
prepared from powder.
At dusk, deacons would string
a bedsheet between the volleyball poles,
a movie projected on someone's
worn 300-threadcount.
Always something Biblical of course:
Jesus of Nazareth, *The Greatest Story Ever Told*,
and, one long night, *Ben-Hur*,
during which most of us kids
fell asleep in rows on the lawn,
still wearing our Kool-Aid mustaches,
too grateful for the long days and freedom
from Catholic school uniforms
to complain about the choice of feature.
But to be gathered up by parents
and grandparents and shepherded home—
that was the closest I ever felt
to being saved.

Mama

My mother is not tall
Or, I guess,
She is tall for a Michoacana,
Towering a full five inches over the abuelas.

In her heels, with her hair teased,
She could almost pass for statuesque.
But with such beauty,
Who needs height?
She had no problem finding a second man
When my father didn't pan out.

How many hours did I spend
Watching her wind her hair around hot rollers
The fog of Aqua Net leaving its metallic tang
In the back of my throat.

I remember the evening gowns,
The peach-colored one with the sequined appliques,
My favorite, because I thought it made her look
Like a Spanish mermaid.

How over the years
We stood at the sink together,
Comparing our hair: Whose was longer.
Whose was thicker. Whose grew faster.

My tias would say, "I don't know how you guys
Can stand it, all that hair. I'd cut it off,
Or at least thin it."

Other women's jealousy is
Something to be cultivated
Like a rare and toxic flower.

Even now,
My mother insists her hair has some natural wave
(It doesn't)
And that mine is finer
(It isn't)

I think, this is the way it should be.
We should all want to be like our mothers.

Until one day, I don't.

I refuse it all.
I let my hair go *toda greñuda*.
I eschew makeup.
I hide my curves in boy clothes
And my face behind books.
Later, I will get tattoos
And a prescription for birth control.
I decide who I reveal myself to
And how much.

I grow to her same height
But otherwise so different;

I take control of my body
In ways she never dreamed of.

Night Song

I am drawn
to darkness and stars,
to midnights and mood indigos,
to the hour of batwings
and unseen howlers.
It's hard to tell, in the dark,
what is menacing and what
is mournful.

Suburban Library

No stone lions,
no columns or mezzanines,
just cinderblock and indestructible carpet,
the place we retreated to
on long, pre-internet afternoons.
The stacks were our ideal habitat.
We went together with books
the way some girls go with horses
or tomboys go with softball.
We won every reading contest,
earned every slice of BOOK IT! pizza,
overidentified with Belle—
not because the local jock was into us, obviously,
but because we talked to clocks,
imploring them to hurry us into adulthood.
Here was the one place we could go
where our curiosity was not met
with strange looks.
Boys, assigned as partners in class,
met us in the study areas.
They didn't know or pretended not to know
how to use the Microfiche or the card catalog
and sat with their feet up while we did all the work.
It was my first after-school job,
and other teenagers, never there voluntarily,
would follow me around, asking,
"So, do you, like, get *paid* to work here?"
Because they could, only too easily,
envision me wrangling books for free.

I bet if you go there now,
you can still find the old bookend
where I scratched my name on the bottom,
my paperback stash in the corner
where I used to hole up
to read during my shifts.
Girls like me read books the way
pilots hit the eject button,
the way the buried alive
claw at the walls of their coffins,
the way young birds leap
from their nests.
We inhabit libraries even as they
inhabit us.

Mi Pelo

Every woman's hair is an epic,
A recording of her life, like tree rings.
Straight, curly, long,
Short, dyed.
The bangs and the layers,
The crimps and the streaks.
Trying to please,
Trying not to please.
The only thing I fret over more than my waistline
Is my locks.

I can't remember a time when people didn't remark on my hair,
When it was not an object of scrutiny or wonder.
Like Jo March, it's always been my one beauty,
Thick and dark.
Too dark,
Or not dark enough,
Depending on who you ask.

Black bobby pins, they said, would not do.
They got gold ones for me instead.
In a neighborhood full of dusky beauties, I was the fairest,
Which is to say, the one who sunburned.

Then we moved to the country, and all the corn-fed
Midwest blondes said my hair was black.
And just like that, I was a crow among the daffodils,
A wren lost in the glare of a sunbeam.

Marooned in the aisle of white-girl beauty supplies
Ponytail holders that could never hope to tame my follicular bulk,
Clips that snapped against the sheer mass
Of its unruliness.

White boys put gum in it, snarled it with briars,
Because they'd been taught that to destroy
Is the ultimate sign of manhood,
And odd-looking girls with unpronounceable names
Make good practice targets.

My hair was straight until I was fourteen.
I slept on spongy pink curlers,
On hard curlers,
Got singed with curling irons,
Endured the chemical assault of salon perms,
Curl-aiding shampoos that made me break out in hives.

Then, mysteriously, it corkscrewed into ringlets.
Perhaps it sought to illustrate the errant thoughts
Teeming in my brain, or God had seen fit
To answer the prayers of my matriarchs,
Gifting at least one of us with natural curls
While the rest of them had hair as straight as Cher's
Back when she still had her Sonny Babe.

Frantically, I tried to comb them out.

The bushier and wilder it got,
The more people seemed to like it
Except for a few critics,
"I don't see what all the fuss about curly hair is.

You really can't do anything with it,"
And "You know, straight hair is *much* more professional."

Random men have come up from behind
And run their fingers through it.
There was a lover who smoothed it back,
Kissed the part, the widow's peak,
And so many women ask me,
What's my secret, how do I
Get it to look like this?

I do nothing. I do nothing.

Once, at a nursery, I found a fern
That felt exactly like my grandmother's hair,
Stiff and raspy along my fingertips.
I refused to put chemicals in it after that.
Later, I learned she teased her hair so zealously
To hide a bald spot in the back.

Now the gray hairs come and I let them.
I will be like one of those old women
Busily selling trinkets outside Cholula,
Restored to my girlhood braids,
Luxurious and white,
But I will be spared the questions.

Kitten Love

There was only one white family on the West Side.
My mother had been friends with their daughters,
and I was friends with their daughters' daughters,
one of whom was this perfect
whiskey-tango beauty named Tish,
who was my first girl crush.
She was 14 and I was 7 and she
had the blond hair/dark roots/dark brows
thing going because it was 1988
and her hair was feathered, of course,
and though we were listening to *Who's That Girl*
I think she was going more
for the Heather Locklear look, and she wore
ragged cutoff short shorts, of course,
threads dangling against her thighs, and she wore
shirts tied up to show off her belly, and blouses
off-the-shoulder, and fringed jean jackets;
anklets and jelly shoes, crooked canine tooth
when she flashed her Lip Smacker smile.
We always used to play in my grandmother's yard,
but if Tish was home, I'd say, "Let's go play at *your* house,"
and Tish didn't mind us kids hanging out in her room.
She would let us sit on her bed. She would braid our hair.
She would paint our nails. We stole one of her
notebooks and found it filled with obscene drawings.
I remember a cartoon mouse with an enormous dick
captioned, *Here, kitty, kitty.*
If Tish ever found out, she wasn't mad about it.
She sat and colored with us, like always,

(non-obscene things, coloring books and crayons
procured at the TG&Y). How gently she traced,
like a kiss, sparkling Tinkerbell lip gloss over my lips.
How she took my hand in hers and whispered,
"Tiny fingers," as she blew
on my still-wet nails.

Working Women

When I was a little girl,
my grandmother and I
would go downtown
to pay the gas
and electric bills.
We'd see those
downtown career women,
in their nylons and walking shoes,
carrying their heels in a purse
or a shopping bag
as they walked to the bus stop.
My grandmother thought
they looked so silly,
in their tennis shoes
and sensible flats,
checking their lipstick
and hair
in storefront windows,
women without men.
My grandmother
never had to walk
five blocks in heels.
She never imagined
being one of them,
but I did.
Now I am
one of those women,
and I am writing this poem,
on a bus,
shoes in a bag
on the seat next to me.

The Page

When I was fourteen, I huffed books.
I sat in the sorting room of the library,
loading up carts, and when no one was looking,
I buried my nose in their bindings.
Not just because I loved the smell of books
but because I wanted to know
where those books had been.
I smelled cigarettes and cigar smoke on them,
I smelled cologne.
I smelled dogs and woodshops, hot glue,
schoolrooms, paint, potting soil,
and, in the case of the old Chilton's manuals,
garages and motor oil.
I smelled spices on the cookbooks and
sweat on the self-help.
I found crumbs in the hinges,
fingerprinted pages, smudges of chocolate,
and far too often, bodily fluids
(which we will not dwell on).
I noted the dog-eared pages,
read the musings scrawled in margins,
triaged the ripped and torn,
tossed heaps of scrap paper
that had served as bookmarks,
shredded old bank statements,
rescued a love letter or two,
tracked down the owner of
an uncashed paycheck
unwisely stowed in the chapters

of a Sue Grafton.
The old checkout system
was already gone,
so I could no longer see
who had read these books before me;
I could only sniff at them,
attempting to track their journey
the way Sherlock Holmes,
with his olfactory genius,
charted London.
The return dates stopped at 1988,
the volumes in my hands
people already thought of
too much as artifacts,
but not the kind I mean—
how I wanted to tell them
what these pages reveal,
how they are the guide and the journey,
the treasure and the map,
the testimony, the evidence, and the scene.
I want them to read what is left in the wake
of this borrowing and returning:
books made of pulp and gray matter,
humans made of dust and dreams.

New Year's Eve Talamada

Needed: at least four women, preferably more.
Abuelas, mamas, tias, vecinas, muchachas.
Corn husks. Maseca. Chili powder.
Papery braids of garlic. Stock.
Slow-cooked pork butt.

Gather in the fragrant and steaming kitchen.
Pour many cups of Nescafe.
Knead the masa. Hands young and old
dip into water, smoothing gritty cornmeal
into a spreadable paste.
Did you hear that Mrs. Diaz kicked her husband out?
About damn time. I heard he's been sniffing around
that prieta that lives over on 17th. What's her name?
Cristina.
Cristina, that's it.

Make the mole. Oil and seasonings coalesce
on the stovetop into a rich, red roux.
Add to pork. *Men are dogs.*
Todos cochinos. They'll stick it in anything.
Pasame la cuchara.

Soak the cornhusks.
Have you seen Lidia lately?
She looks awful, just wore out,
like she's been rode hard and put away wet.
She can't be that old.
Yeah, but after six kids? It's a wonder

the flaps of her panocha aren't dragging along
on the ground behind her, like a damn parachute.
Remember how pretty she used to be?
Never a hair out of place.
You wouldn't know it now, to look at her.

Shred the pork. After simmering all day,
it should be so tender, it practically swoons
beneath the tines. *Alice Flores called yesterday.*
Her oldest boy, Roman, is back in jail.
What for this time?
Pues, ¿qué piensas tu? Para drogas.

The long task of rolling,
daubing the husks with masa.
Fold in meat and seal neatly.
No one wants a messy tamal.
And what about you, mija,
when are you going to get married
and start having babies?
You know, Manuel always liked you.
He's got a good job.

Line the bottom of the pot with the broken husks.
Waste not, want not. Steam about 15 minutes
or until masa is firm and dark.
There's a New Year's resolution for you:
try and make yourself more appealing.
You don't want to end up like poor crazy Yolanda.
Never married. The neighbors say they can hear her
up there, talking to herself.
One of those lesbians, if you ask me.

If there is leftover mole, pour over top.
Serve hot. Men and boys eat first.
Eat up, mija. But tomorrow, you should go on a diet.
You're starting to get a big culo.

Handwash Only

When I think of winter,
I think of the heaps of laundry.
Bulky clothes making
for more loads,
more hours spent,
taking things in and
pulling them out
of the machine,
the 100% wool sweaters
that must be washed
at the kitchen sink.
I think of the drying rack
I unfold in my kitchen,
trying to spread out
as many sweaters as I can
along its aluminum arms
to let them drip-dry
onto the linoleum.
I think of a childhood friend
whose father raised sheep,
the time I saw the flock
huddled together in a snowy pasture,
a cloud of fleece,
black faces a perfect contrast
to the whiteness surrounding them.
When I put your Irish sweater
up to dry, I can still smell the farm,
woodsmoke and lanolin.

The Art of the Backyard Haircut

Two barefoot children
The adjacent lot vacant
Separated by the warped diamonds
Of drooping chain link

A neighborhood of pitted driveways
And muddy porches,
Of bikes propped against the sides of houses

They drag a patio table
Into the center of the yard
Items balanced carefully on its surface:
Comb, brush, shears, electric shaver
The ashtray where their mother parks her cigarette

The boy can hardly stand still long enough
To have his hair mown down to prickles
Through which the white of his scalp shines through.
At the back of his head is a whorl where the part would begin
If he had enough left to part,
Exposed ears translucent as elm leaves.

The girl, far less certain, clutches a princess doll,
Her mother's fingers move through her locks like sunlight
The snip of the blue-handled scissors soothes and satisfies,
Cross-eyed, the girl follows its journey across her forehead
An instrument forbidden to little hands,
The same twin blades that cut twist-ties on hanks of lettuce,
Or the thread of a Thanksgiving Day turkey.

Afterwards, they check the straightness of her bangs
With a schoolhouse ruler.

Newly weightless, the children run,
Heap of hair scattered to the grass
By the winds of their departure.

Piojos

I told you to keep your heads apart.
Didn't I tell you? Ay wey, hold still!

In days of sleeping eight on the living room floor,
Eating together, bathing together,
Contact is inevitable.
It becomes a habit, to scratch our heads
And immediately check beneath our nails
To see if we've unearthed anything
Squirming and multi-legged.

Now the house is redolent of bleach,
Towels and linens soaked in hot water
And hung out to dry in the sun,
The hairbrushes collected in the sink,
Vacuum humming as follicles are slathered
In pesticide shampoos.

The worst part isn't the itching
Or even the ick factor.
It's that there's so much standing still involved:
Ten minutes for the treatment itself
Then the long task of combing out nits.
My hair takes longer than everyone else's. I have so much,
And it's the same color as the lice themselves.
My aunt, mother and grandmother hover,
Passing the comb back and forth as they take turns
Going over it.

As with most things, the boys have it easy.
Their heads are simply shorn, and in no time,
They're back at the pool,
Doubly cool for summer months
While I sit in the steaming house,
Preparing for another treatment.

Why can't we cut off my hair? I ask.

Because, they sigh. *It's too pretty.*

DeeJay Love

Sixteen years after Buggles' one-hit wonder,
we were still smacking snooze-buttons on clock radios,
jarred awake by Top 40 and traffic on the nines.
We listened on the bus going to and from school.
We listened in the locker room.
We listened at each other's houses.
Our moms listened in the kitchen, our dads in the garage.
It was the noon, the five, the after-dark, the love lines,
the weather report, the advice, the Casey Kasems,
the Howard Sterns, the college stations,
the underground, the AM strangeness.
It was the seventh-caller concert ticket giveaways,
the whatever's-below-the-D-list celebrity interviews,
jingles for local eateries, cheap auto insurance,
guitar stores, used car lots, tanning salons, and head shops.
Our idea of interactive was to call in during request hour
and dedicate a song to the boy we liked in class,
"I'll Make Love to You" or "So Much in Love"
(the All 4 One version, as if it needed to be said).
And, at the center of it all, the deejays,
the princes of the airwaves.
Was it any wonder we got crushes on them?
A particular type of crush, the kind
that can only develop when you can't see them
and they can't see you.
On a dare, I called one up and talked dirty to him.
Hey, baby, I said. *Your voice gets me so hot.*
You know what really turns me on?
I was thirteen. This is girl bravado,

the way that boys will take a baseball bat and smash a mailbox;
they toy with destruction while we just self-destruct.
I hoped the deejay was recording me,
that he would play our conversation on the air.
My heart was beating so hard, and my friends
were giggling and shushing each other behind me,
so I didn't hear his response. But I lost my nerve,
and just before I slammed the phone down,
I yelled, *Play "Trigger-Happy Jack"!*

Large-Breasted Woman

No matter what you do, you cannot escape this décolletage.
Such a frank manifestation of sexuality cannot be repressed,
like a female baboon's cinnabar ass. No amount of layering,
no stifling sweatshirts or severe-necked blouses,
no knee-grazing t-shirts can convincingly shield.
Not even the standard-issue garments distributed
by the world's virtue police can successfully stifle
that which is determined to stick out.
You were the first girl in your class to need a bra,
and not even the training variety. Somehow,
overnight, you went straight to a B cup.
So when the boys should've been watching Reading Rainbow,
their gazes were drawn to the strap sliding down your arm.
How embarrassed you were to be seen strumming it back into place
with a sad little note, your shoulders like the knobs of a lyre,
enduring the other girls' scrutiny and dismay.
People who've never gone through it can't imagine
the pain of those buds forcing themselves out,
the literal pain, stretch marks splitting flesh.
People who've never gone through it can't imagine
such exposure. Everywhere you go, boys want to grab them,
even gay boys. In your twenties, you go to drag bars,
thinking it's got to be some kind of safe space,
but the queens' reverence for tits is its own weird thing.
You learn before you even have words for these kinds of encounters
that the body is a betrayer. People think the contours of your sweater

spell some sort of promise. This is how it starts:
this slouch, this erasure, until you're just the thing they hang on,
like a coat tree or a scaffold. By middle school, they're so big,
they brush your arms. When you walk, you can feel every jiggle.
Gym class is a theater of agony for most people anyway, but not
like this,
not a locker room full of eyes watching you change out of your
sports bra
and apply Lady Speed Stick to the undersides. You dread the
summer,
navigating its cuts, sleeveless and backless and halter.
How you want to resist, how you cling to your tomboy card,
pitching softball and climbing trees, going au naturale
until the other girls sneer and say, "Put on a bra, slut.
You're bouncing around all over the place."
Your first real tube of lipstick was Rum Raisin.
When you wear it, gazes linger. You shave your legs for the first
time
and a boy at the pool wrinkles his nose and says, "You're all
stubbly."
By the time fall rolls around again, him and his bros will have the
lingo down:
Bitch. Butterface. On the rag. On the street outside Dairy
Queen,
a man growls, "You a stallion, girl. I could ride you all night long."
And what is there to do but run home and rub the lipstick off?
What is there to do but to lower your voice, your eyes,
your expectations? You try going skinny, learning how to survive
on one meal a day or less, hoping for some shrinkage, but these
mammeries
have a mind of their own, jutting out further from your
diminished ribcage. So you go the other way, eating and eating,
which doesn't work either, because fat girls give the best head,

fat girls are like motorbikes, fat girls have rolls everywhere
that are like bonus boobs. The men who fancy themselves sophis-
ticated
inform you that the female body is art, so really,
you're a masterpiece, baby. How great men would have salivated
to capture your form in plaster and marble and paint. It's roman-
tic.
It's a compliment. Say thank you.
When a co-worker asks you to run away with him,
that's a compliment, too. When an old high school classmate
stalks you on Facebook. When a man threatens to kill himself
if you won't be his. Don't you know? This is why
girls like you used to get tossed into Magdalene laundries. Girls
like you
still get tossed onto honor pyres. People think that menstruation
is the curse of Eve, but really, having bodacious tatas is the real
curse.
These dirtypillows, twin sins spilling out of a V-neck,
and your back and shoulders will attest to their devilry. Now,
a wife for nearly twenty years: the cropping up of silver hairs on
your scalp,
the softening into matronhood, mom jeans hitting
well above your belly button, and something your dermatologist
assures you
is a liver spot. This is the blessed waning of attention, these dugs
finally achieving their biological function, the sustaining
of a child. You look back on old photos and see yourself,
marveling at how young you were, and wonder, how,
even with those lips and those DDs, anyone could ever
have mistaken you for anything but the girl you were?

Nuestra Señora de Ogilvie

In summer, the women in my family gathered
Like Cezanne bathers or Florentine graces,
Stacks of tabloids and magazines at the ready,
Radio tuned to the AM Spanish station.

My aunt did everyone's hair in the kitchen sink,
Scooping water over foreheads,
Encased to her elbows in yellow gloves.

Not too curly, hija,
I don't need no damn Afro.

Bottles of dye and boxes of Ogilvie home permanent kits;
Baskets of rods—
Afterwards, the house will be littered with them,
Freshly chemicalized black hairs still clinging to pink plastic.

In their chanclas and faded house dresses
They'd go out onto the porch, settle down in the open air,
Oddly regal with their hair wrapped, turban-like,
In towels or shower caps,
Chatting over their reading material,
Shouting the occasional greeting to neighbors.

I gravitate towards bottles of nail polish,
The many colors and tiny brushes,
The sharp scent of remover.
I ask my abuela if I can do her toes.
No, you'll just mess it up.

So I do my cousin's instead,
Alternating pink and red.
We see only the fun of camaraderie.
We don't understand this is the price women pay,
A sacrifice to whatever ammonia-smelling goddess allots desir-
ability:
This effort,
This time.

Fondant

For many years, my mother baked cakes as a side business.
It brought in very little money, but it united her love of baking
With her love of working with her hands.
Our house smelled perpetually of vanilla and sugar,
The kitchen sink overflowing with flowers to be crystallized,
Like scrubbed young women waiting to be transformed into brides.
She made sheet cakes and groom's cakes, shower cakes, petit fours,
And once, a lady's social club requested an assortment of delicacies
To be served at high tea.
Given a picture and a recipe, my mother could make anything.
Customers would sit in the living room, sipping coffee
As they discussed flavors and the number of guests.
My mother even gave demonstrations on the proper way
To cut and serve. As with everything else,
There's an art to it: one by two inches, economical and democratic.
Our countertops were littered with the tools of her trade:
Pans, tiers for stacking, lifters, little green baskets of berries,
Toothpicks and popsicle sticks for propping and holding things in place,
Toppers, pots of paint in case she needed to touch up a face,
To turn a plastic blond into a brunette, or vice versa,
Icing bags and tips, and of course, there was always cake.
There was always an assortment of frostings, bricks of cream cheese,
Fairy mounds of powdered sugar, Play-Doh-like fondant.

The cobbler's children have no shoes,
But the baker's children can no longer abide buttercream.
For my birthday, she always asked me what I wanted,
And I always said, a plain Bundt cake,
Which I never got. It was always layers and scalloped frosting,
A message written in a flourish, *Happy Sweet 16,* or
Sure do love you. I didn't realize
She always saved her best work for us,
I didn't think about the joy she gave people,
Underscoring the sweetness of their occasions.
But when she made my wedding cake, she knew
I didn't like almond, so it was a strawberry-swirl dream
Beneath its beautifully molded trappings, and of course,
I botched cutting it, the piece I fed to my husband uneven,
At least four inches wide. To this day, I can barely stand cake.
Now her things sit in a storage box in the basement,
All those shining white and stainless-steel implements
Gathering layers of dust for ten years.
Arthritis. Carpal tunnel.

Pan Dulce

Someone remarked to me
that Mexican pastries
are not very sweet.
It's because
they're meant to be
dipped in chocolate
or café con leche,
I explained,
the traditional
Mexican palate
does not hold
with too much sweetness.
But, as my grandmother
pointed out,
that's a lie,
the advent
of Coca-Cola
and Snickers bars
turning everyone
fat and diabetic
in no time.
She's not wrong,
her own love affair
con cosas dulces leading
to a lost hand,
dialysis.

Hoop Dreams

Mi bisabuela got her ears pierced
at two days old. Who knows
who actually pierced her tiny
infant lobes—her mother,
a midwife, a neighbor,
almost certainly a woman.
After one ear had been pierced,
she kicked and squirmed,
so the second piercing
went askew. She was sixty-five
when I came into being.
Whenever I picture her face,
I always see her crooked earrings,
how one always sat a little higher
than the other, her lobes creased
with age and nascent heart disease,
a winking pair of pale blue
aquamarines in a silver setting.
My mother and grandmother
tried over and over to pierce
their ears, but it wouldn't take.
When I was born, my mother waited
till I was two months old to try,
desperate for me to have
all the giant gold hoops,
big enough for a parakeet to perch on,
big enough to fit a regulation
basketball rim, all the flashy
diamond studs, all the drops and dangles,

all the filigree, plastic, novelty, buttons,
all that bling she and my grandmother
had been cruelly denied.
It didn't work for me, either.
We tried again when I was eight,
then again at fifteen.
The holes always closed over.
They exchanged looks over
my head and nodded sagely to
each other. "It's the German blood.
Has to be."

Languages, First and Last

You were four
When you came to this country.
Shame was the first lesson.
Being neither black nor white
Meant you were welcome nowhere.
There were no ESL programs in those days,
So English was not optional.

By the time you were fourteen
Your accent was long-gone.
You sounded just like any other Midwest girl,
With blurred vowels and dropped G's.
You ate hamburgers and mashed potatoes
And adapted to snow,
But there was no hiding that black hair, that brown skin.
It was easier to pretend you were Italian,
To pepper your speech with *arrivedercis*
And hang out on the east side with Joe Church's boys.

At sixteen
You birthed your own true-blue American
But gave her a red-white-and-green name.

At thirty-nine
The grandchildren began to arrive.
They had names like Robert and George.

At sixty-three
Great-grandchildren,
Of which I was the fourth.

You called me *mjia*.
At the market, you would point.
I would say, *manzana, pollo, papas.*
You would say, *¿Que color?*
I would say *roja, blanco, marròn.*
You would point to yourself and I would say, *morena.*
You would point at me and I would say, *gringa.*

When I was seven and you were seventy-two
I refused to answer you in Spanish.
My stubbornness held out till I was twelve
And you were seventy-seven.
I was too young to understand that heritage
Is not a hobby. It's not something you can just put down
And pick back up again at your leisure.
I was too young to understand that a tongue
Is also a root. What nourished and sustained you
I thought was dust, so I spat it out.

When I was seventeen and you were eighty-two
I spent a summer in Madrid. You were so proud.
You loved my Castilian accent, my postcards of the Escorial,
My recipe for *tortillas españolas.*

When I was twenty-two and you were eighty-seven
You couldn't understand the Indian doctor's accent.
Then you ceased to understand the nurses, the hospice workers,
The soft-spoken priest.
On good days, you thought I was my mother.
On bad days, I was just some white girl.
Names, English, eighty years—
All of it had faded, as if you'd already returned
To that bygone place.

When I was twenty-five and you were ninety
You died.

Now I am thirty-four
And there's no one to call me *mija.*
Sometimes, I still dream in Spanish.
People I feel great tenderness towards,
I call by Spanish names;
In moments of great distress,
I revert to your exclamations, *¡Ay, por dios!*
¡Que pendejado!
But I can barely roll my r's anymore and I no longer
Check the bilingual box on job applications.

And yet, I had you longer than you had Mexico.
If I live as long as you, then I will have had
Sixty-five years to lose and reclaim
A tongue, a nation, an identity,
A root, a history, a shrine,
A refuge,

You.

Rootstock

My grandmother lived in a shotgun shack.
She was not like other grandmothers.
She was a recovering alcoholic on disability
with a string of broken marriages behind her.
She did not speak softly.
She did not bake cookies.
She did not knit.
She certainly didn't garden.
Yet there were fragrant climbing roses in her front yard,
crimson with gold centers. They bloomed once a year,
early in the season, in time for us to trim a bouquet
for May devotions to the Blessed Virgin.
We had no money for a vase, so we used an orange juice can
that we decorated with construction paper.
It was the only time we ever did something like that together.
We were so proud of that bouquet, certain that Juan Diego himself
would have gathered those roses into his cloak
and declared a miracle.

When the roses passed, they littered the sidewalk
with their once-velvety petals, their leaves gone to black spot.
For the rest of the summer, Grandma would trim the cane
just enough so that it wouldn't overtake the porch.

Later, I learned that those roses are only good for rootstock.
Someone had planted them with hopes for better things,
but they wouldn't stay underground, especially now
that whatever horticultural prize they were meant to bolster

is long gone, and those roses continue to thrive,
to bloom, to climb, to suck
the soil
dry.

Unused

The piano sat in the sun room
beside a potted tree,
fall board raised only once or twice in my lifetime.
Curious, I had fingered the keys.
I asked my grandfather if we could have it tuned
so I could take proper lessons.
He said no.
When he died, I returned
to a musty carpet and faded cushions.
Dead olive leaves curled among the strings,
their crackle the only music beneath
my dumb fingers.

The Ledger

I have dealt with death before.
All my grandparents have passed away.
There was everything leading up to their passing,
Then the mourning, which everyone knows,
Never really ends. It's just something you learn to carry.
Then I watched my parents go through all the practical hassles
Of settling the estate: planning and paying for funerals,
Insurance, probate, managing medical bills,
Selling the houses, hauling furniture out to the curb.
A veritable slog of phone calls and paperwork.
Even now, eleven years after my grandmother died,
A life insurance policy we never knew she had
Has surfaced, a small pay-out that has to be distributed.
But this is the first time I've had to do something
Even remotely close to this.
The vet gave us a quote.
The appointment has been set.
Now, as I go over the monthly budget,
I realize I need to add a line item,
But I can't bring myself to write it in.
I will wait until afterwards.
I will label it with her name.

Dear Abuela

Every day, I miss your kitchen,
its odors of garlic and cumin,
watching you roll tortillas,
grate cheese for enchiladas.
I miss the shaded patio, the side garden,
staked tomatoes growing heavy and red on their vines,
fragrant bunches of mint and cilantro.
You told me I must always wash my hands
after picking peppers, but I forgot
and rubbed my eyes. You held my head
under the faucet in the kitchen sink, where,
a few years before,
you had bathed me as an infant.
I miss the rain, how we used to watch it
pour from the eaves.

Low

It is a testament
to the universe's cruelty
that a woman who underwent
a hysterectomy at age 26
now has a belly
as round as a melon.
No one warned her
about this rearrangement,
a sort of visceral musical chairs:
Your intestines hang low now,
the doctor says.
You'll never have a flat stomach again.
Adhesions snake
their insidious loops,
tugging, squeezing,
long nights clutching
a heating pad.
The pain of absence.
The pain of being filled.
The pains did not go away.
They're just different now,
along with going through life
looking perpetually pregnant,
even though she is
curved
and empty
as a rind.

Sidekick

If this were a movie, I'd be the sympathetic best friend,
pudgy pushing towards matronly, but unfailingly cheerful,
endearingly clumsy, utterly unfashionable.
Whenever the Hot Main Character goes through a crisis,
she'll be able to call me or just drop by, no matter the hour,
and I'll be there, waiting for her with tubs of ice cream, chick flicks,
and the appropriate wisdom: *Follow your dreams.*
He's not good enough for you, or, *Yes, he's flawed,*
but you two were MADE for each other. Go get him!
And I would not be allowed a love interest,
at least, not at first. My tummy and thighs exist
only to make the hot girl look hotter, the way that Ethel
had to be ten years older than Lucy;
I would be the sensible, bespectacled Velma to her leggy Daphne,
both Selma and Patty to her Marge Simpson.
But in the end, when I am a bridesmaid at her wedding,
I'll finally be allowed, as an afterthought, to meet someone.
He'll be as chubby as me, bearish, maybe a beard,
definitely jolly. Our eyes will meet over the buffet table.
I'll probably even still be holding a chicken wing in my fist.
We'll smile bashfully and hopefully.
My face will be smeared with teriyaki sauce.

Nameless

Dear Nameless One, Dear Not-Daughter,
I hold your secret name close to my heart.
How clearly I used to imagine the prefect blending
of your would-be father's features and mine
that would one day be your face;
how one day you and I would dance around,
singing, "Penny Lane." Day by day, I feel you
slipping further and further away. I don't know
how you can be a ghost since you never
lived in the first place. I can only see you
up to about twelve or so, and then you fade,
and I fade, and I regret having no tears for you.
All the salt has been leached from this body,
all anima ceased in this soul.

Inheritance

Sometimes, I wonder
what I would've taught
my grandchildren.
My own grandmothers
were not like
everybody else's grandmothers.
They cussed and brawled and
got thrown in drunk tanks and
told dirty jokes and laughed
raucously and wore
lots of eye makeup.
I like to think
I would teach you
the grandmotherly things
that I've read about:
how to bake cookies,
how to collect buttons in a jar,
how to reuse margarine tubs
instead of Tupperware.
I don't know how to quilt
or knit or anything,
but I do know
how to love fiercely,
unapologetically,
and to be who I am.
I like to think
I would have
passed that along
as well.

Sleeping Alone

My mother suffers
from nightmares
and chronic pain.
Almost 65 years
of wear-and-tear
and untold traumas
driving her to sleep
on the sofa,
where she can brace
her body against
the backrest,
to prevent her
from rolling over
and re-awakening
old hip and shoulder injuries;
she drifts off to the flicker
of History Channel
pseudoscience documentaries
and midnight reruns.
I try to convince her
to smoke some weed
to soothe her many hurts
but she says no.
The old stigma
is too embedded,
and besides, she watched
three brothers succumb
to their chemical demons.
So she sleeps alone

in the living room
where my step-father's rest
won't be interrupted
by her nightly cries.

Waiting

Four months and eight visits to the ER.
After that, you stop counting,
or forget how to count. Anyway,
you're on a first-name basis
with the intake folks, and make jokes
about having a bed on reserve:
Garcon! Where's my phlebotomist?
I insist she attend me at once.
Once again, I watch them wheel him back
while I am left to deal with the paperwork.
Later, inside the corpus of the hospital itself,
mammoth, shifting organism of renovations
and walkways, I wander 2am visitors' lounges,
vacant except for doctors and nurses
in their sneakers and scrubs, trying to perch
on uncomfortable sofas and chairs,
trying to catch forty winks between shifts,
the night nurses who move silent as specters
through dim wards, checking vitals
and IV bags. The cafeteria, shuttered and scoured,
where a bank of vending machines lights up
at my approach, like an alien greeting.
This is the desperate hour, meals of
plastic-wrap chicken salad and empty calories
you don't taste. The unreal hour,
balanced between life and not-life,
but you don't know which is which.
The panic hour, where your sobs
are just another echo inside the beast.

Comfort Animals

That time when you were still on dialysis
and my parents took us to the zoo to cheer us up.
I don't know how long you'd been on it at that point.
It didn't take long for it to feel like forever.
You were so weak, you had to walk with a cane,
so we rented a wheelchair at the admissions booth
and I wheeled you around all day.
We visited the kangaroo field and the penguin house.
We fed goats and leaned over simulated tidepools
to fondle sea urchins and starfish.
Whatever year it was, most people
had already graduated to smart phones,
but we still had flip phones because
nothing induces poverty like medical catastrophe.
So we wrote down our animal-related questions
on a notepad to look up later on the internet.
We learned all the fun facts like
giraffes have black tongues
and tigers have striped skin,
vampire bats regurgitate and share blood
to help their sick,
deer continuously shed and regrow their antlers,
certain species of lizards can regenerate their limbs,
and dolphins have been known
to lead other species to safe waters.
We bought a hot pretzel that I ended up eating
because you had no appetite.
I spent so much of that time
worrying about you not eating.

Hyenas eat bones, hooves, horns and hair.
And all the people smiled at us,
me for being the good and dutiful wife
and you because I'm sure they were
all imagining that you'd been wounded
in Afghanistan or Iraq,
because that's how people of our age bracket
usually end up in wheelchairs,
and I want to tell them that man
didn't do this to you. God did.
But I just keep smiling, and we have ice cream—
that you do eat, though the phosphorus is bad for you.
Later, we learn some jellyfish are immortal,
that gibbons, wolves and bald eagles
are among the creatures that mate for life,
and sponges that are divided
can grow back together again.
And my parents were right.
We were comforted.

Spirit Death

Dawn never feels
like a beginning
anymore.
Only the beginning
of the end.
Some days, I wonder
if I died in my sleep
and my spirit just hasn't
figured it out yet.
Today, from the bus,
I saw a woman collapse
against the wall
of the hospital building.
Her grandson had to
hold her up.
I'm tired, she kept saying,
I'm just so tired.
Her world had clearly ended
and her spirit knew it.

Chasing Grace

This is how I handle myself:
gingerly, then roughly.
I am a pilgrim within my own body,
looking for something to hail.
The beautiful girls walk by
and I am the unholy ghost
at their well-turned heels.
They don't see me go out
with my compass and lantern,
searching for some
overlooked relic.
Then I remember
that I am not dead yet.
These knucklebones are still
firmly attached.
I am attached to the hands
that are both the seekers
and the sought-after.
What secrets might my entrails spill?
I try to be careful, but I am
increasingly frantic,
cuts appearing and deepening
in this desperate claw
through the thorn bushes
on our way to grace.
O Lord,
this dermis is so heavy.
I long to lift it like a skirt
and run.
But I'd only trip
on my way to meet You.

Montego Bay

For thirty-three years, your exposure to water
consisted of quarries, creeks,
and the occasional lakeside barbecue.
Life on the transplant list kept you grounded,
so this was only our second seaside vacation.
You came prepared with beach shoes,
a swim shirt because the anti-rejection meds make you
high-risk for skin cancer, and snorkeling gear.
I was in awe of your fearlessness as I watched you suit up,
your scars hidden beneath blue Lycra.
I am not fearless. I stayed on the shore,
content to let the waves wash over me,
and sift handfuls of pebbles through my hands,
turning up only cockle shells and broken scallops,
watching you swim farther and farther out.
You were determined to explore a reef that lay
somewhere beyond the buoys.
Before I knew it, I could barely see you.
You can't imagine the panicky flutterings,
as if I'd swallowed live kelp,
akin to watching you get wheeled off to the operating room,
glaucous hospital light a universe apart
from the blue Caribbean.
I carry it with me forever, that light,
the way I will carry forever the flash of sun on your fins,
how, in that moment,
you were closer to the horizon than you were to me,
how you dove.

Chaos Theory

One winter,
a freak wind blew
the scent of pigshit
from farms in Nebraska
two hundred miles south
so my street was suffused
with the stink.
I hear it wafted
all the way down
to the Ozarks.
I keep thinking about
ill winds
and how shit
rolls downhill
and when a pig
gets slaughtered
somewhere outside Lincoln
thunder shakes Mountain Home
and I pull my scarf up
over my nose.

The Macaws

Mi abuelo brought a pair of scarlet macaws
back from Mexico one year. I imagine he thought
their rainbow-colored plumage would help carry him
through the bleak Midwest winters, a reminder of home.
He a built a cage for them of scrap lumber
and chicken wire and put them in the sun.
He fed them a rich diet of fruits and nuts.
Yet, they squawked all night long,
even when their cage was covered with blankets.
They had been wild-caught,
and never stopped honking their outrage
for the loss of their tropical nativity, for lychee and guava,
for eggs that Abuela didn't carefully boil
and slip back into the nest of newspapers
beneath the female's tailfeathers. Instead, they had fleas,
a corner of the living room with its wood-paneled walls,
a single maiden-hair fern in macramé,
and a view of the blue-collar street beyond.
The floor around their cage was covered
in walnut shells and rinds and shit.
In the summer, they were moved to the back porch,
and one day, fed up with avian infanticide and sleepless nights,
Abuela left their cage open. Now, I see news articles
about parrot colonies from Miami all the way to New York,
birds of paradise roosting in palm and oak alike,
thriving anywhere that gardeners offer up flower
and fruit trees, power lines succumbing
beneath the weight of their nests, whole electrical grids
wiped out by their persistence of being, while back in the tropics,

deforestation is killing their kind. And then I understand
why Abuelo related to these birds so well:
in a new country, he found a bed, a mate, the flower,
the fruit, and the meat of the nut. He found a way
to birth generations.

Moving Day

Everything packed and loaded
into the car,
including the bird feeder.
As I walk through the old place
one last time,
I see the birds gathered on the porch,
singing for a supper
that will not come.

Found Photos

Our little town had a newspaper
founded in 1846.
Its offices were on the square,
where we used to wander as teens,
aimless, sullen,
buying lattes and Italian sodas
at the coffee shop.
There was a water fountain
outside the newspaper office
that drew us,
and we lingered to look
at the unclaimed photos taped to the window,
like lost baggage at the airport
or rental storage units
delinquent in their payments—
you wonder what's inside:
white-framed Polaroids,
rectangular One Hour Photo prints,
engagement and wedding photos,
studio portraits,
black-and-whites presumably
for the obituaries
showing the local departed in their heyday
all beehives and pincurls,
ruffle-throated powder-blue tuxedos,
navy uniforms.
There were shots of track meets,
of flood damage,
of atmospheric conditions,

purple-green tornado skies,
snowed-in streets,
store grand openings,
award-winning flowers,
prize cows,
little miss competitions,
karate tournaments—
the story of a town's life
laid out like an autopsy.

I don't know how long the photos
stayed in the window.
Some of them had been there so long,
their tape had started to curl up around the edges.
I, too, would have been hard-pressed
to throw them away,
those little celluloid echoes.

The paper shut down two years ago,
but I still think of those forgotten faces,
those forgotten situations.
In antique stores, I look for stacks of photos,
treasure troves stowed in old hat boxes
or tied with twine.
At used book sales, I fan the pages out,
sifting like an archaeologist at a dusty site,
hoping for postcards sent from another time.
I examine them, trying to recover
the lost afternoons,
an answer to all the question marks
punctuating my own life,
forgotten doors, wormholes,
signposts on the way to eternity.

The Nostalgia Project

When my mother and stepfather downsized
from the house I grew up in to something
befitting retirees, there was almost forty years
of stuff shoved in basements and closets, despite
diligent garage sales and trips to Goodwill.
A heap of old photo albums came to me,
lone survivor of so many deaths, divorces,
and remarriages, a final loop of wool
in an otherwise unraveled garment.
One album went back to the 1920s,
with edge tabs and black pages,
falling apart, lost photos leaving behind
ghostly windows, all the faces unknown to me.
Others were from the 70s and early 80s,
sticky, yellowing leaves that have lost
their adhesiveness, whose cellophane sleeves
have grown loose and crinkled.
Some of the photos themselves are faded or scratched.
I dutifully begin scanning them so they can be
easily shared with distant relatives, to see if anyone's
memories reach back that far, files labeled
and sorted to the best of my knowledge. I will
transfer the photos themselves to new albums
to try to preserve the original snapshots and Polaroids.
Twenty albums take me months to get through.
At the same time, I think, mere months
to preserve the artifacts of at least five generations?
That something that's supposed to be so permanent
and historic can be so easily undone?

Surprise Blooms

Another new place, another new yard.
No matter how carefully you inspect,
there are always surprises waiting
in the lathing and frames:
a window that always sticks,
a cantankerous sink that spits scalding water,
a bloom of mildew on a basement wall.
In spring, one can expect beds
of ragged perennials around the hedges,
some unkempt bulbs,
an unsuccessful herb garden
where the spearmint persists,
but what of these long stalks
springing up here and there on the lawn,
where the grass gives no hint
of former landscaping?
Like discovering bones of unknown soldiers,
buds unfurl flags of a forgotten nation,
pale pink, a faint tinge of blue.

Saffron

It's hard to imagine how
once I stood half a world away
from where we would meet,
looking out over saffron fields.
All summer long, I watched
the low green plants
poke from sandy soil,
but I would be gone
before the crocuses
could bloom, exposing
by night their
coveted red stigmas.
I would never have
the orange-stained hands
of a mondadora.
Now, as many years later
as my age that summer,
you buy a bottle
of the expensive spice
with just a few threads inside
like a witch ball,
and serve me paella
in our own kitchen.
One day, you promise,
you'll give me back
La Mancha.
With my mouth
full of rice,
I believe you.

Running Barefoot

It's been said that
Couples who've been together a long time
Begin to resemble one another.
These cracked heels and leathern soles will attest:
They've been kissing ground
For quite some time.

A Jazz Fable

after *Count Basie and the Kansas City 7*

It feels like a fairy tale
(What'cha Talkin)
to imagine
my grandparents
young and hep
my grandfather
a handsome rogue
in a fedora and chalk stripes
my grandmother in
long beads and high heels
and they were the couple
that all the other couples envied
going to see
Bennie and the Count
(Tally-ho, Mr. Basie)
down on 18th and Vine
swilling bathtub gin
(Senator Whitehead)
couldn't stop 'em
it was a wide-open town
dancing
(At the Count's Place)
swing stomp and ragtime
till dawn broke
over old Electric Park
and she was just 16
and her dress was blue

and she was a child bride
(I Want a Little Girl)
and her bruises were blue
and her sorrows were blue
and her suitcase was blue
and there was no one
to tell her
(Secrets)
to
and she fled to Chi town
just like Basie
when the band broke up
to sample
what freedom had to give
on the banks
of Lake Michigan
(Oh, Lady, Be Good)
but dreaming
of the riverlands.

Sunday

The eve of the work week,
and we must prepare
for the time ahead,
for the time that
is not our own.
These ablutions,
how they consume,
these puttering Sunday afternoons,
when the house smells richly
of your cooking and baking bread
while I do laundry:
unfolding the drying rack,
running to and fro with the basket,
cats circling my ankles.
The air steams with boiling pots
and hot water cycles.
After dinner,
you fall asleep early,
your head in my lap.
This would be our moment,
captured in amber
or a snowglobe,
sparkled flakes falling around us
as I look down at you,
your eyelashes dark in the lamplight,
your hands, still dusted with flour,
curled beneath your cheek.

Prodigal

Homesick, I conjure memories
of Heartland springs: the scent of silt loam,
of river bottoms, of the golden sedge and wet
prairie cord grass. The petunias are beginning
to overflow the barrel planters. I could bathe
in the evening lilac, I would lie down in my tracks
for the invasive honeysuckle, its promises
a lull on my tongue. I like to think that,
somewhere, a grove of pin oaks
craves my footsteps, that limestone paths
have recorded my rambles and play them back
on an endless loop, that the feathery moss
trembles for the embrace of my shadow.

Getting Settled In

New house, new stove,
and you,
swearing at the burnt bread.

Return

In the old neighborhood, I walk. I return
to the scenes of my beginnings. Heroes
get origin stories. Characters
get backstory. We get only
decaying houses, an empty pool
where we used to swim
in little-girl bathing suits.
Mine was pink with stars.
It's drained now, my water,
while my stars overflow
with my adult body. I remember
how I once slipped and scraped
my knees on this playground.
My skin is a part of this place.
I am a part of this place. I am
a part of something. It is a part
of me. These connections reawaken
like old neural pathways lighting up again,
like old streetlamps with new bulbs
burning brighter. Nearby,
I rent rooms where I live. We'll call it
a home. I fill the tub. Fluttering shadows
of birds and butterflies come in
through the blinds. In the water,
I feel their shadows through the glass
like a weight across my skin.
They are descendants of old birds
and butterflies that have touched me before
with their shadows. You can drink
from the same river twice. You can
go home again.

Publication Notes

"Paper Wasps," *Ponder Savant, The Art of Depression* series, July 2019

"A Feast for Mosquitoes," *Duane's PoeTree Blog,* June 2019

"Abuela" - *Peinate: Hair Battles Between Latina Mothers & Daughters* anthology, September 2018

"Deep Creek" - *Heliopause Magazine,* Issue 2, December 2018

"Jesus Flicks" - *The Wild Word,* Issue #41, *Long Summer Nights,* July 2019 (Germany)

"Mama" - *Poetry Breakfast,* November 29, 2017

"Night Song" - *Stanzaic Stylings,* March 5, 2019

"Suburban Library" - Featured Reader, KC Reach Out and Read Librarian's Club Happy Hour event, November 4, 2019; poems posted on KC Reach Out and Read website, November 2019

"Mi Pelo" - *Mermaid Mirror: An Anthology of Women Writers,* edited by Adam Levon Brown and Chani Zwibel, Madness Muse Press, February 2018

"Kitten Love" - *Mojave River Review,* Spring/Summer 2019

"The Page" - Featured Reader, KC Reach Out and Read Librarian's Club Happy Hour event, November 4, 2019; poems posted on KC Reach Out and Read website, November 2019

"New Year's Eve Talamada" – *Otherwise Engaged: Northern New Mexico Literature & Arts Journal,* Vol. 3, Summer 2019

"The Art of the Backyard Haircut" - *The American Journal of Poetry,* Volume Three, July 2017

"Piojos" - *Peinate: Hair Battles Between Latina Mothers & Daughters* anthology, September 2018

"DeeJay Love" - *Herstry,* December 2018

"Large-Breasted Woman" - *Flint Hills Review,* Issue 23, July 2018

"Nuestra Señora de Ogilvie" - *Into the Void* (Canada), Issue 6, October 2017

"Fondant" - *Sheila-Na-Gig,* Vol. 2.4, Summer 2018, Special Feature: Poets and Editors

"Hoop Dreams" - *Barren Magazine,* Issue 11: *Bifurcate,* October 2019

"Languages, First and Last" - *The Voices Project,* May 2016

"Rootstock" - *Brenda, BLOOM* (UK), Issue 2, August 2018

"Unused" - *Warriors with Wings: The Best of Contemporary Poetry* anthology, edited by Michael Lee Johnson and Ken Allan Dronsfield, July 2018

"The Ledger" - *Thimble Literary Magazine,* Vol. 1, No. 3, December 2018

"Dear Abuela" - *Peinate: Hair Battles Between Latina Mothers & Daughters* anthology, September 2018

"Low" - *Anti-Heroin Chic,* March 2019

"Sidekick" - *Sheila-Na-Gig,* Vol. 2.4, Summer 2018, Special Feature: Poets and Editors

"Nameless" - *Black Coffee Review,* Fall 2019

"Inheritance" - *The Gasconade Review,* Ladies' Night issue, December 2019

"Waiting" – *The Literary Nest,* Vol. 5, Issue 1, Spring 2019

"Comfort Animals" - Winner, Seamus Burns Creative Writing Competition (Northern Ireland), November 2019; to appear in *The Honest Ulsterman* (TBD)

"Spirit Death" - *Sleet Magazine,* Millennial Edition, January 2020

"Chasing Grace" – *Panoply,* Issue 13, Summer/Autumn 2019

"Montego Bay" - *Willawaw Journal,* Spring 2018, Issue 3

"Chaos Theory" - *Re-Side,* Issue 3, Winter 2019

"The Macaws" - *The Gasconade Review,* Ladies' Night issue, December 2019

"Moving Day" - *Ariel Chart,* January 2019

"The Nostalgia Project" - *Stanzaic Stylings,* March 8, 2019; also printed in *Duane's PoeTree Blog*, March 2019

"Surprise Blooms" – Change Seven Magazine, TBD

"Saffron" - *Heliopause Magazine,* Issue 2, December 2018

"Running Barefoot" - *Five : 2 : One, #thesideshow,* February 2018

"A Jazz Fable" – *Artifact Nouveau,* TBD

"Sunday" - *Inverse Journal* (India), February 2019

"Prodigal" - *The Conclusion Magazine* (Bangladesh), Vol. 2, December 2018

"Return" - *The Wild Word,* Issue #41, *Long Summer Nights,* July 2019 (Germany)